Nostalgic

Nostalgic Memories

A Collection of Lancashire

Dialect Poetry

Jeff Unsworth

Copyright © 2021 Jeff Unsworth.

The book author retains sole copyright to his contributions to this book.
All Rights Reserved. No part of this book may be reproduced, except for the inclusion of a brief quotation in review, without permission in writing from the author/publisher.

www.jeffreyunsworth.wixsite.com/wigandialect

ACKNOWLEDGEMENTS

To Barbara for the patience, encouragement and constructive criticism she has given over the years and whilst this book was being compiled.
Also for her kind permission to use photographs from her family collection.

To Karen and Julie, who were the first to encourage me to write these poems.

To Bethany, who encouraged me to publish this book.

To Karen for her help with the proof reading.

****

This book is dedicated to my paternal grandparents Joseph Unsworth & Esther Wadsworth/Unsworth and my maternal grandmother Annie Seddon/Gardner. It was from them that I picked up quite a great deal of Lancashire Dialect and a lot of the content of my poems is directly related to my experience of them and the way they used to live and speak.
Some of these poems contain mild

expletives but I decided to leave them in to stay true to the way that they spoke.

Whilst there is a small amount of poetic licence used in the poems, the majority of the content is how I remember it as a child growing up in the 40's and 50's.

Jeff Unsworth

INDEX

11. Th'istry Of Wiggin
14. Wiggin Pier
16. The Story of Mabs Cross
20. Hard Wark
21. Posh Visiters
23. Aspirations
25. Canine Wishes
27. Blast From The Past
29. Jeffrey's Catty
31. Ceawnt Thi Blessins
32. Cowd Cure
33. Conveners Address
34. Likkle Jim
35. Miss'in Th'owd Cock
37. Wash'in Mi Hair
38. A Nip I'nt Th'air
39. Visit'in Mi Gron
41. El Toopay
42. Scithers, Combs un Pensuls
43. Gradely Meyt
45. Goo'int Baths
47. Th'olidays
48. Shill'in for Cleun'in
50. Th'only Solution
51. Womtime at Golstones
52. Worr a Palava
54. Th'Unsworth Dragon
56. Mi Kin
59. Pick'in Coal
61. Faythers Day Eawt
63. Old Pictures

TRANSLATIONS

65. Translations
67. The History of Wigan
70. Wigan Pier
72. The Story of Mab's Cross
76. Hard Work
77. Posh Visitors
79. Aspirations
81. Canine Wishes
83. Blast From The Past
85. Jeffrey's Catapult
87. Count Your Blessings
88. Cold Cure
89. Conveners Address
90. Little Jim
91. Missing The old Cock
93. Washing My Hair
94. A Nip In The air
95. Visiting My Gran
97. El Toopay
98. Scissors, Combs and Pencils
99. Good Food
101. Going To the Baths
103. The Holidays
104. Shilling for Cleaning
105. The Only Solution
106. Home Time at Golstones
107. What a Palava
109. The Unsworth Dragon
111. My Kin
113. Picking Coal
115. Fathers Day Out

INTRODUCTION

I was born in No 55 Tram St, Platt Bridge, near Wigan, Lancashire in 1946.
Having been raised in a place where dialect was a normal way of speaking, it was natural to pick up words and phrases that for many people have long since become redundant.

Not wanting these dialect words and phrases to disappear and to keep the memories of where I originated, I decided to commit some of what I remembered to verse for posterity.

After writing a few verses over a number of years, I entered a local Festival of Arts competition in 1996. I entered a very short but funny poem entitled "El Toopay". To my surprise, it won 1st prize in the humorous section. It was at this time that I decided to compile a collection of dialect poems.

This compilation of verses is not meant to be an in depth study of Lancashire Dialect but a collection of situations and events that I hope will bring a smile to the readers face.

I realise that dialect is difficult to read or

understand. Therefore I have included translations to each poem. These can be found in the last section of the book.

Please bear in mind it is not always easy to translate each word or phrase without losing the rhyme.

Jeff Unsworth

Jeff Unsworth

Th'istry of Wiggin

Wiggins bin ere a reight good while.
Abeawt 2000 ere or so.
Thowd name of Wiggin wuz Coccium.
A name not mony folk know.

Th'origin of Wiggins a mystery.
Though we know that Romans were ere.
Cos when thiv bin digging a few holes in't road.
Thiv font a few things ere un theer.

Th'istry's a bit muggy arreawn't miggle ages.
Un't writins are not very thorough.
But we do know some time abeawt 1246
King Henry he made it a Borough.

Neaw Wiggin, this new Royal Borough
A Proud Teawn of eawses un farms.
Reflected it's status laahk other big teawns
Un gett'n it's own coat of arms

Dur'in Civil war Teawn wuz royalist.
Support of King Charles a matter of course.
Commander er't forces, the then Earl of Derby
Made Wiggin th'eadquarters er't force

Neaw.. Parliamentry forces of Bowt'n.
Captured Wiggin un looted through't teawn
Demolish'in fortifications.
Which simply means wars were knocked deawn.

Cromwell hisell headed troops.
In 1648.
Un went into battle at Standish.
Which turned into a nasty greyt feight.

On't banks of't River Douglas.
Shed blood would leave its stain.
It entered the local folklore
As the Battle of Wiggin Lane

The Earl of Derby, James Stanley
Notoriously known as Lord Strange
Was arrested and convicted of treason
An execution was quickly arranged

His death it occurred in Bowt'n
Eawtside of the pub Man & Scyth
Theres a plaque that still marks the spot where he dee'd.
The place wee'r he ended his life.

Wiggin also witnessed the very last act.
In th'istory of the Stuart cause.
When Bonny Prince Charlie after lois'in at Derby.
In Hallgate he stopped for a pause.

Century after century as time went on.
Wiggin grew some moo'er.
Th'industrial Revolution ,
The teawn an opp'n doo'er.

Canals & pits and factries
Springin up reawnd here.
A teawn that's full of humour.
Wi it's famous Wiggin Pier.

Many famous folk and things.
Has put Wiggin on the map.
Like Orwell, Formby & Randell.
And of course the owd flat cap

Rugby League & footbaw
Barges filled wi coal.
The Verve and Wiggin Casino.
Th' heart of Northern Soul.

Wiggin a thriv'in werk'in teawn.
Yo only af't oppn your eyes.
A teawn thats known for awsoats.
Not just pratuh pies.

Wiggin Pier

George Orwell wrut a book, tha knows,
The road ter Wiggin Pier.
He tried fot tell it eaw it wuz.
Un eaw folk lived reawnd here.

He tried fot give a detailed view.
Abeawt th'unemployed un't poor.
He even lived among um aw.
Fot help im larn some moo'er.

He wrut abeawt aw't miners.
What their werk wuz laahk.
Worr a poxy darty job it wuz.
Enough fot mek thi skraahk.

Conditions were'nt reight gradely,
Werk'in undergreawnd.
Hot un cramped un dusty,
Wi not much room fot turn'in reawnd.

Tunnels, oney three foot heigh
Werk'in on their bally's.
Picks un shovells, scrawp'in coal,
In order't get their tally's.

They trudged wom in their pit dirt.
When their shifts were done.
It were ard fot tell which wuz thi Dad,
Black faces, every one.

Stripp'in off their darty cloo'us.
Gerr'in in't tin bath.
This is wee'er yo'd see aw't scars,
The pit faw aftermath.

Dark black lines across their backs,
Wee'er coal geet under't skin.
The wives would scrub
But neyer would they be laahk what they'd once bin

Condemned eawses, Orwell wrote.
Areawnd th'area of Scholes.
Four rooms, two up two deawn.
Sometimes flea ridden holes.

Leak'in roof, walls faw'in deawn
Un damp in moo'ist er't bricks.
Windows would'nt opp'n reet.
Rent six bob un rates at thee un six.

Poverty wuz rife, George Orwell wrote.
Thirty theawsund claim'in dole.
Tha were fain if tha'd even geet a job.
Even digg'in coal.

He wrote mortality wuz very heigh
Un illnesses were rife.
Un generally or't folk areawnd these times
Had a really awful life

The Story of Mab's Cross

Poem inspired by the account written by

Frank Hird 1910

....

Sir William Bradshaw of Haigh.
A knight of some reneawn.
Wed a young wench fer Blackrod & Haigh.
On theawtskirts of owd Wiggin Teawn.

Sir William…He a't go away.
Fo't feight in some ere waar.
It met er bin Bakkle er Bannockburn.
Or it could er bin further afar.

Neaw, it's said he wuz tak'n pris'ner.
But what we don't know is, eaw lung.
Aw we know is he ney'er come wom.
Abeawt that thi cor'nt be far wrung.

Anyroad…Ten ear went past.
Un William, He ney'er come wom.
Un Mabel think'in him dee'ud.
Startid knock'in abeawt wi this mon.

Apparently. There'd bin a rebellion.
Agen Edward the second, no deawt.
Un this ere welsh mon cawed Osmund.

Wuz in his good books,for help'in him eawt.

He reakoned he'd bin granted possession.
Of Haigh Hall. Well that's worr he said.
Un Mabel her at fot move eawt.
Unless her accepted fot wed.

Neaw… fot save her'sel and her childer.
From beggery un financial ruin.
Her at use her noggin un feminine whiles.
In short…just waatch worr hers doin.

Her wuz forced into marryin't Welshmon.
Lady Osmund Nevill, her title.
Her could'nt do nowt abeawt it.
Safety er't fam'ly were vital.

At theend er ten year or so.
Her were dolin eawt bread, one fine day.
When one mon approached for his shive of bread.
Un revealed, he was William of Haigh.

Neaw, Mabel her recognised William.
In shock, her lerr eawt a scream.
Un Osmund when he heard abeawt it.
He grabbed her and smacked her reawnd th'een.

Neaw, William, He bided his time.
His bite, wuz wuss than his bark.
Un then he waylaid Welshmon, Osmund.
Un kil't him eawtside Newton Park.

The troubles of William and Mabel.

Were nor ore, one as't for say.
For slay'in the welsh knight at Newton.
William was eawtlawed a year and a day.

Neaw, Mabel for unwitted bigamy.
Even in spite of her loss.
Aa't walk barefoot from Haigh Hall to Wiggin.
Each wik, to a place cawd Mab's Cross.

When his outlawry was ended.
William went back to his kin.
Un when he dee'd, Mabel ordered.
A chantry building for him.

Eventually, her dee'd an aw.
Un in that chantry, both lay.
Yo con see it, if yo go't Wiggin.
Cos theyre tombs are still thee'r today.

The legend of Mab's Cross dates from 1295 when Sir William Bradshaigh married Mabel

Norris de Haigh. According to the legend, William was away at war for so long, that Lady Mabel assumed him dead and married a Welsh knight, Osmond Neville.

After seven years Sir William returned, in disguise. He fought the Welsh knight at Newton Park, Newton-le-Willows and killed him there.

As penance for her unwitted bigamy, Lady Mabel walked barefoot each week from Haigh to the cross in Wigan Lane, which then became known as 'Mab's Cross'.

The stone cross probably dating from the 13th cent is located in Wigan Lane, Wigan.

The remains of the cross are a one metre square dressed gritstone block 0.57 metres (1.9 ft) high on top of a stone plinth

It was originally one of four stone crosses used as waymarkers along the medieval route from Wigan to Chorley. The cross no longer stands in its original position, having been moved across the road in 1922 as part of a road widening scheme.

The tombs of Sir William and Lady Mabel are located in Wigan Parish Church.

Hard Wark

Owd mon, as't at sit mi deawn.
Mi legs thiv varneer fawd off.
Mi feet are both warchin, wi runnin abeawt.
Un I think that wiv aw done enough.

Worreyer we do , they'll want moo'er.
Their rulin aw't factry wi fear.
I don't care eaw soon it gets orf past five.
Un then wi con gerr eawt of here.

Av neyer met no'bdy us likes it.
Un folk , they keep grip'in aw day.
They sey that were wark 'in ar fingers ter't bone.
Its not wuth it for what bosses pay.

But there's nowt that wi con do abeawt it.
We aw av fot carry ar load.
Thiv gett'n us aw ore a barr'ul.
Cos nobody else pays thi road

Posh Visiters

"Were goo'int av cump'ny today
Neaw a wa'ant yo do what yo towd
I don't wa'ant yo manki'in abeawt
Burr I wa'ant yo be as good as gowd".

Aunty Winney it wuz uz wuz com'in
The one whose eye all'us flickers
Everyone thowt her wuz posh
I reckon it's fur coat, un no nickers

Neaw,we add'nt much jackbit in't pantry
So mi mam made a plate praytuh pie
"Ickle be awreet", her said, "wi some carrots"
"That er'd be grand" answered I.

"For afters we'll have jelly un custer't"
Her said wi her best'ist posh voice
"Un av made a nice Sing'in Lily
So that Winney has gett'n a good choice".

I said, "Mam it's like hav'in a party"
Un it did look a reet gradely pie
"Aah, well that's goo'int cause us a problem"
Her had this sly look in her eye

"There wain't be enough pie for aw of us,
Cause that's aw jackbit win gett'n.
So Jeffrey, when I ask if tha waants some
Say no'w tha nor hungry, tha's ett'n".

Anyroad..

Visitors sat deawn for dinner.
Un then the pie was fotched eawt
I wuz aggrovated dee'uth
Cos I knew I wuz goo'int go beawt.

"Would you like some pie, our Jeffrey,
You know it's your favorite" she said.
"No Mam I'm not feeling hungry"
When really, I could have ett'n a flock bed.

I sat theer while everyone ett'n
Think'in of nowt but the sweet
A greyt bowl of jelly un custert
That surely would make things awreet.

" Con I have some jelly un custert , Mam"
I asked with a glint in mi eye.
"No…you can't" was the answer.
"You would'nt eat any of the pie"

Aspirations

Ah'm leav'in skoo on Friday.
Aah'v geet misel a job.
Aah'm start'in i smithy come Monday.
For a wage of thirt'y bob.

Tomorrow aas't at go't serp'lus store.
Fot get some hob nailed boots.
Un then aah'l waant an avasack.
Un one of them theer, beyler suits.

Aah did'nt waant fot go in't factry.
Un definatly not deawn pit.
So av geet misel an apprenticeship.
But mi fayther, he did'nt laahk it.

"Norr as much money as they gerr in't factry.
Tha knows"
Un they'l tak thi forr a foo.
As soon as tha's done serv'in thi time.
Tha'l eend up back in't dole queue".

"Chep labour that's what them jobs are.
Aah'm tell'in they ickle come to neawt.
Thaah should have come ter't Maypow.
Where aah could uv sort thi eawt"

"There's no way thill get me deawn't pit.. Dad
Aah'm beawnt bet'ther misel one day.
As soon as aah come eawt mi time.
Aah'l eend up on full pay.

Aahs't av mi own eaws one fine day.
Un aah'm goo'int av a car.
Un as't tak mi childer for an oliday.
Someweer further afar.

Aah'v norr had much in't way of thing.
Un as't at do it misel, it seems.
Burr aah'v geet mi yed screwed on reet road
Un besides…Aah'v geet mi Dreams

Canine Wishes

Kids ar maahther'in for a dog tha knows.
Ax'in every day
Their plagu'in mi't dee'uth abeawt it.
Aahm goo'int at gee um their way.

Aahm not keen on gerr'in one misell.
Tha see's……. aaahv had one afoo'er.
Chew'in aw through't furniture.
Un pee'in aw or't floo'er.

Ikkle be a novelty for a couple er wik.
They'll bi walk'in it abeawt.
Then soon they'll aw bi sick of it.
Ikkle me us'll at takk it eawt.

Dogs are not forr eawses…. Aah don't think.
Slavver'in aw ore't floo'er.
Dragg'in it's backside alung best rug.
Un scratch'in aw't back doo'er.

Sniff'in other dogs backsides.
Then lick'in thi on't face.
Runn'in in when it's pour'in deawn .
Un stink'in eawt front place.

Un then it's cost er feed'in it.
Un wi'st at bey it a baw.
Aah mean…them two dogs on't mantlepiece
Don't cost nowt at aw.

As't at get Charlie Hines fot dock it's tail.

Then mek sure it dunt get fits.
Un then theres things laahk worm'in it.
Un then aw't thuther bits.

Aahm beawnt at put mi foo't deawn.
Un then that will be that.
Un if thi keep on skraahk'in.
Aah'l think abeawt a cat.

Blast from the Past

Whilst maw'in abeawt in't back yard.
Me un ar kid wuz digg'in up seyl wi a stick.
When wi font this owd rusty hand grenade.
It were nesslin under this brick.

"What we goo'int do wi it?", ar kid said.
Cos wid neyer seen one like it befoo'er.
Neaw wi at fot be quiet at this point.
Cos grandad wuz oppnin back doo'er.

Neaw grandad wuz owd'in his papper.
He passed us, un gee us a smile.
We knew he wuz goo'int ter't petty.
So we knew he'd bi theer for a while.

Wi waited till he geet settl't deawn.
Thrutch'in un fart'in, he wuz.
Norm'ly tha'd keep weel away.
Stink'in the way thad he does.

It's a rusty owd sod, this hand grenade.
As we examined this thing that wi'd feawnt.
Just then our kid poo'ed this pin eawt.
Then clod it…. un started fot ceawnt.

It rolled deawn ter't bottom er't yard.
Ar kid, he went whaah't as a ghost.
It eended up a midges frum lavvy.
Weer grandad sat read'in his post.

Our kid.. he start'id a skraahk'in.
He'd av gett'n it back if he could.
But then nowt app'nt for a minute.
It wuz then that wi thowt it a dud.

WHEN…..

This thing, it went off with an almighty bang.
Clouds of muck, dust and smoke….. What a state.
We both were frickn'ed and started fot run.
And then we saw grandad, hanging ore't gate.

Laughing his yed off, our grandad was.
And then through or't laughter, he said.
" I wonder what this gran er'd have thowt.
If I'd let one like that go in bed".

Jeffrey's Catty

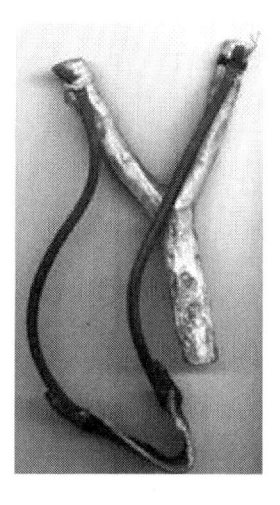

Aah'm beawn't mek a catty this afty.
When aah get wom fer skoo.
Lastics brock'n on't thowd un.
Un av not gett'n much else fot do.

Aah'v sin a belt'in two leg.
On a tree in Leylund park.
Aah'm goo'int go deawn thee'r at orf past six
As soon as it's gett'n dark.

Mi dad se's av not fot aah one.
Cos aah kil't a sparrow.
Burr he'l not know thar av geet it.
Cos aas't hide it under't barrow.

Aahm bestist shot in Higher Ince, me.
Aah con hit a con at thir'ty yard.
Aah con hit a gas leet at fifty foot.
Un't th'arse er't next doo'ers cat is not so hard.

When aah'v geet mi two leg.
Un two foot of square lastic.
Aah'm beawnt cut tung eaw't of mi shoe.
Cos things, they get that drastic.

Yo see, Aah need a leather pouch.
Un there's no wee'r else fot go.
So aa'st at keep hid'in both mi shoes.
Then mi dad u'll neyer know

So neaw av geet mi two leg.
Some lastic un tung eawt of mi shoe.
Neaw I need some cott'n.
Any colour u'll do.

Aah'l nick some eawt mi mothers tin.
There's no way of her know'in.
Un if her thinks there's not much left.
Her'l think her's used it sew'in.

Aw't th'ingreediunt neaw av geet.
Aah'm ready fot drive folk batty.
So folk,waa'tch eawt cos Jeffreys here.
Un Jeffreys geet a catty.

Ceawnt thi Bless'ins

It ses in't Bible not fot envy,
All'us waant'in worr others av geet.
Fot be fain wi what tha's bin gin.
Un trust it'll aw be awreet.

There's all'us sombdy wuss off.
Us is in a wuss state than thee.
We aw should ceawn't ar blessins.
Un think that could av bin me.

There's days that we aw get brassed off.
Wish'in we ad a bit moo'er
But there's plenty of folk us has gett'n nowt ey't.
Un there's them us as't sleep on't floo'er.

Tha only as't look reawnd abeawt thi.
It's thee'r for evryone't see.
We aw should ceawnt ar blessins.
Un think that could av bin me.

Whenever we're feelin a bit deawn.
Not thankfull the way that we should.
A walk reawnd a ward deawn at Christies.
Er'd do us a reight world er good.

Stop skraakin un think thisell fain.
That's the reet way fot be.
We aw should ceawnt ar blessins
Un think that could av bin me.

Cowd Cure

Crin, aah'v gett'n a yedwarch.
Aah think aah'm cotch'in flu.
Aah'v takk'n a couple er Beechums.
Aah'm op'in that they'l do.
Aah trey'd a couple of asprins, fust.
Burr aah could'nt shake it off.
Neaw mi nose is runn'in.
Aside frum that, aah'm startin't cough.

Aw mi bones are warch'in.
Aah'v ulcers on mi gums.
Aah'm goo'int av a whiskey.
Or else a couple er rums.
If aah ad'nt geet faws teeth.
Aah'd swear they aw were ach'in.
Un't wife, her's geet no sympathy.
Sez her corn't bi doo'in wi aw this neyse aah'm mak'in.

Her sez aah should stop skraahk'in.
Which dun't orf get me raahl't.
Her sez tha dun't know what suffer'in is.
Until tha's had a chaahl't.
Eeh.. ecky thump, aah'v start'id sweat'in.
That rum, it's start'id werk, aah think.
So bugger aw them tablits.
Aah'l av another drink.

Conveners Address

" Reet lads , we'll have a meetin."
Is usually the sheawt.
" Wiv geett'n a bit o bissniss,
We'll at get sortid eawt.

Awt lads ,they start a gathrin,
Un meetins on the go.
Un then we hear them famous words.
" Reet lads. Us yo know."

Meetins cawd to order.
Un soon gets under way.
Un then Convener tells us,
Were on abeawt ar pay.

" Eaw much ar they offrin."
One mons er'd fot sheawt.
" Is it wot we ast for,
Or are we cummin eawt."

" Neaw calm deawn lads,
There's no talk of us straak'in.
Fust, lets consider worr thiv offered.
Afoor we aw start skraak'in.

" I'll read yo wot thiv offered then.
Burr a want yo keep yo cool.
If yo don't like wot yor ear'in.
Yo con allus werk to rule.

Likkle Jim

Bah thi eck it looks a seet
Deawn yon Shuttle street.
Chances of gerr'in it clean is rayther slim,
Wi only one sweeper. Likkle Jim.

It's funny it's not made im bitter,
Eaw folk keep clodd'in deawn ther litter.
Burr he just keeps goo'in from yer to yer.
Mind thi. Thats wot they pay im fer.

Walkin deawn at mornin .
After Sunday neet.
Tha wants to see awt papper.
It dunt orf look a seet.

Eshpeshly if it's windy,
Mekin it look wuss.
Burr it neyer bothers Jimmy.
Yo neyer ere im cuss.

He just plods on from day to day,
Wi his spade un likkle brush,
Goo'in alung at an even pace,
An neyer in a rush.

It's " Mornin Mary,
Eawt goo'in on Bob."
Un then he gets his yed deawn.
Un carries on wit job.

Miss'in Th'owd Cock

"Wot's up we yo mother.
As summut geet yo deawn.
Yo favver yuv font a thrip'ny bit
Un lost an hay'f er creawn"

Eeh!
"Am just sut ere on mi own
Think'in abeawt thowd lad.
Aay.. Aah wish thowd cock were ere neaw.
Then things would'nt seem so bad.

Aah used gerr on at im, tha knows.
For breyk'in wind un stink'in.
Aah'd gee owt neaw, fot hear im fart.
Un aah would'nt mind im drink'in.

Aah'd luv be tuck'in his shart lap in his drawers.
Un mek'in sure his fly was done up.
Un tak'in him bed when he geet wom at neet.
Aw them times he'd ter much fot sup.

Aah would'nt complain abeawt muck on his lap
Or't snot that was aw deawn his sleeve.
Or in't latter days when he pee'd deawn his leg.
Aah just wish't thar he did'nt at leave.

Aye!
Aah wish't he was here we us neaw.
Un then aah could kiss his bawd yed.
Aw't things aah wish't ad er towd im.
But neaw …. it's too late fot bi said.

It dun't seem two tics sin he popped his clogs
Laah'k Darby un Joan we used fot be.
Un neaw…when aah think abeawt thowd lad.
Aah wish the Lord er'd tak me.

Neaw, come on mother,buck yo'sel up.
Dwell'in on it's beawnt be upsett'in
Un yo know just wot mi fayther er'd sey.
Neaw, Esther, thee stop thi frett'in.

He would'nt waant yo sut abeawt mope'in.
Yo know just worr he'd say.
Come on ar Ace. gerr off thi backside.
Un make us a nice cup er tay.

Waash'in Mi Hair

Aah think al wash mi hair ter neet.
It's gerr'in full er dir't.
It's full er muck un dandruff.
It's faw'in on mi shirt.

I don't like lookin scruffy,
So while Iv'e gett'n time.
I'll gi mi hair a reet good scrub,
Un hang it eawt on't line.

This Poem was included in an English Educational Textbook, designed to help 11-14 year olds improve their speaking and listening skills and to introduce them to the study of spoken language.
Published March 2011.

A Nip I'nt Th'air

" Mornin lads, it's not so waarm."
Is usually the greetin.
When't werk'ers enter Golstones,
Un place it still wants heatin.

Better leave thi coat on ,
Until tha's ad a drink.
Un then wil see shop steward.
Un he con cause a stink

" Ar lads wain't werk in this ere cowd."
Will be the plea from him.
When really it's nor aw that bad.
Well. Not for werkin in.

Wee in an har, it soon gets waarm.
Un so yo see it shows.
A likkle bit of awkertness,
Ull keep um on their toes.

Visit'in Mi Gron

I all'us visitid , Set'day.
Fot do shopp'in for mi gron.
Platt Waz wuz a lung way for chider.
On't trolly buz , from bird ith ond.

It seemed a lung way in them days.
When thar abeawt nine , er ten.
But two an a tanner wuz too much fot miss.
Tha could buy awsoats for thripp'nce back then.

Neaw I coud'nt abide peylin praytus.
As a chilt, it fair geet mi deawn.
But mi fayther , he said I at do it.
If I wa'ntid fot get orf a creawn.

Sumtimes ad stop theer ore neet.
It were beltin, come time fot gut bed.
Wid clamber upstairs wi a candle.
Which flickered on faythers bawd yed.

Wid aw av a pee in'tert jerry.
Which was quickly shoved back under't bed.
Tha could smell it in't neet if tha wack'nd.
But nothin abeawt it was said.

Wid lie theer wit candle a flickrin.
Makin shadows un shapes aw oat war.
Un wid play at tryin't find faces.
On't damp patches that we aw saw.

When time come fot bi goo'in.
Mi gron said.. " Joe , trait that lad ".
But mi fayther he all'us at plague mi.
Which used get mi gronmother mad.

He'd sit on a cheer , wi his back fac'int fire.
His braces were danglin ter't floo'er.
He'd say.. " Jeffries , come poo mi finger.
Then fart, un I'd run eawt er't doo'er.

He'd give me the money , I'd kiss im on't yed.
Mi gronmother see'd mi ter't doo'er.
I'd kiss her on't cheek , her'd give mi a hug.
I'd say.. " thanks , un I'll see yo some moo'er.

El Toopay

It startid wi a bawd spot,
Abeawt as big as orf a creawn.
Then it gett'n bigger,
un werk't its road areawnd.

Every time I ad a bath,
or washed mi hair at neet.
I'd look deawn on'tert floo'er,
There'd bi hair aw reawnd mi feet.

Faw'in eawt in chunks, it wuz.
Bawd as a coot , on top.
Un then I tried a Toopay,
Favver'd a flamin mop.

I said I would'nt wear it,
Wife said, it looked awreet.
I said us folk erd laff at mi ,
becos it looked a seet.

Her geet her road, I wore it.
It were stuck on wi tape, un pinned.
Burr everybody laffed at mi.
It blew off in't flipp'in wind.

This Poem was the winning poem in the Leigh
Festival of Arts Dialect Poetry Competition 1996
(Humorous Section)

Scithers, Combs un Pensuls

I corn't find them scithers.
Av bin look'in for an har.
Has any er yo lot sin um.
They corn't er gone so far.

There wonc't were tharteen pair in this eaws.
Kept I yon sideboard.
Just wait until I find um.
As't hide um eawt er't road.

Its same wit combs un penculs.
There's all'us faw'in eawt.
Cos when tha comes fot wa'nt one.
There's neyer noan abeawt.

Sumb'dy ul cop it one day.
Tha'l hear um sheawt eawt " owch ".
Then tha'l know thiv font um.
Thi'l be deawn back er't couch.

Gradely Meyt

It's ard fot understond dialect.
Ikkle surprise mi if tha con.
Cos theres cert'in things that's said reawnd here.
Tha corn't mek yed nor tail on.

I mean, eaw con't expect a southerner.
Us is in a queue wi us.
Understond when some yowth asks.
For two un orf peawnd er praytus.

Neaw.. folk up north are gradely.
Un by God thi know eawt eyt.
Cos thowduns learn or't younguns.
Eawt cook a piece er meyt.

Theres Tripe un Brawn un Wessun.
Lambs Fry un Slavvery Duck.
Theres Ceawheel un sometimes a nice sheeps
yed.
Wi't legs wi any luck.

Theres Elder, Pigs Cheek un Trotters.
Oxtail un a nice bit er tung.
Burr it's moo'istly thowduns that eyt it.
They'l not touch it when theyre young.

Today they know nowt abeawt cookin.
They gerr it aw eawt of a con.
Or else theyre defrost'in a packit.
Thowd road of cookin is gone.

In't thowd days, nowt gett'n wasted.
Ballyhond day, in't miggle er't week.
Aw't left ore's geet clod in a greyt fry'in pon.
Un come eawt as Bubble un Squeek.

Toad in't th'ole, Lobbies un Broth.
Else bakin till aw hars er't neet.
Jackbit that went a good way.
Were't th'answer for mek'in theends meet.

Tha could'nt blame really.
It were hard fot mek them eend's meet.
They did best thi could, with what they could get.
Un moo'ist were run off theyre feet.

I look back sometimes ter't thowd days.
Un although there were'nt allus Mey't.
I remember there were allus jackbit.
We allus had summ'ut fot eyt.

Goo'int Baths

It were beltin goo'int baths on a Set'day.
Three or four of us waitin fot buz.
As soon as it come, wid aw feyt gerr on.
Cos aw of us wa'ntid bit fust.

Neaw sumdy all'us fogeet summut.
A towel , there'd be a fair chance.
But we neyer forgett'n ar cossies.
Cos we ad um on under ar pants.

Afoo'er buz stopped , top o King Street.
Wid jump off , cos we aw could'nt wait.
Wid leg it through Grimes's arcade.
Cross Library Street, into Millgate.

Neaw .. by this time wid aw be excitid.
Racin ter't bottom ert slope.
Then beawncin through dorr , wid aw get that
wiff.
Of chlorine, un carbolic soap.

Three of us squa'shed in one cabin.
Gerrin undressed , stood on't seat.
Then beltin deawn steps inter't shars.
Lathrin ar cossies , un scrubbin ar feet.

I wonc't geet clod eawt for pee'in in't pool.
Thatendunt he pooshed me in't road.
I said it were'nt reet .. us moo'ist folk pee.
He said .. " aye " but norr off top divin board.

Neaw.. they'd clod us aw eawt abeawt four.
Wid wunder weer time it'd gone.
Wid caw in a shop for an hovis breawn loaf.
Un e,yt miggle eawt as we walked wom

Th'olidays

I'm fain it's gett'n tholidays,
I'm just abeawt gerr'in sick.
I corn't say its rest i'm need'in .
Burr a breyk for a couple er wik.

As't bi flirt'in off to Blackpoo,
In a nice ot'el as guest.
Burr I bet when fort.nits ore,
I'll be glad get back werk fot rest.

I ope we get good weather,
Burr it'l prob'ly rain aw wik.
Un kids u'll aw be skraak'in,
We'll aw be gerr'in sick

Then wife, er'll start complainin,
Un wish we adn't come.
Un then I'll prob'ly leyse me rag
Un whip um aw back wom

Shill'in for Cleeun'in

Reet… Were goo'int go through th'eaws today.
Aah want th'whole place clee'un.
Yo not goo'in play'in till it's bin done.
So aah ope yo aw know worr aah mee'un.

Neaw thee Raymund, thaa con do't petty.
Get Lanry from under yon sink.
Un mek sure tha scrubs under't lavatry rim.
It's that whats bin caus'in that stink.

Terunce, thaa con do grate.
Gee it a reight good black lead'in.
Un mek sure tha cle'uns inside er't thov'en.
Even if tha as't get thi yed in.

Scrawp aw them clinckers from th'esshole.
Then opp'n that new bungle er sticks.
Screw up some papp'er fot mek a good fire.
Cos thi dad'll bi wom abeawt six.

Jeffrey.. thaa con do kich'un.
Un don't thee forget stone that step.
There's a new donkey bran under't slop stone.
Un tha knows wee'er mop rags are kept.

Aah'm beawnt fot go an fill't dollytub.
Theres a greyt pile er waash'in waants do'in.
So while am in't waasheaws, no faw'in eawt.
Neaw pick up yo things un get goo'in.

Oh…un one of yo u'll at turn yon mangle.
Cos aah corn't do them blankits misell.
Un as't waant a lift wi pegg'in um eawt.
If their not back on't bed..He'll play hell.

Aah ope av geet time nip ter't popshop.
Cos as't at gerr his suit eawt agen.
Un then it waants spong'in un press'in.
Un then he'll not know weer it's bin.

So come on lets aw get stuck in.
Aah waant yo aw show will'in
Un if we get done afoor he comes wom.
Aah met trait yo aw to a shill'in.

Th'only Solution

Nineteen yer owd, un sut in't theaws.
Its norr her fawt, her corn't gerr a job.
Its gerrin ter't state where hers willin tak owt.
Just fot mek a few bob.

It corn't do no good for kids at her age.
Sittin for ars, writin page after page.
Applyin for this, un applyin for that .
Then earin hers bin turned deawn flat.

It meks thi wunder wots goo'in on.
Un wot there aw goo'int do.
They keep on seyin educate.
They'll at stop on at skoo.

But road that I understond it.
There's only one thing fot do.
That's lowerin retirin age .
Deawn to twenty two.

Womtime at Golstones

Gerr eawt road, ther com'in.
At orf past three , they sheawt.
It's murder if tha copped in't rush.
When't wimmins comin eawt.

Aw that bumpin weight.
Feightin 't get tert front.
There's one theer . must be twenty stone.
Favvers an elefunt.

If tha gets in't road er yon yowth.
Underneeth them legs.
Tha'l eend up in Leyth I'firmry'
As sure as eggs is eggs.

So tak a tip from one us knows.
Un lissun to this line.
Try gerr eawt afoor um.
Else werk some o'ertime.

Worr a Palava

Worr a palava at bedtime.
Three grown up folk un four childer.
Two double beds un one single
No wonder mi mam was bewilder't

Neaw mi nana her at likkle bed.
Un mi mam un mi dad had a double.
That left oney one moo'er fot childer.
Un that's why we ad aw this trouble.

We tried aw roads fot sleep we some comfert.
Length ways un crossert's we'd lie.
There were elbows un legs aw ore't show
It were easy get poked in thi eye.

"Stop turn'in o'er" one er'd sheawt eawt.
"Gee us some blankit" skraahked another.
Get thi elbow eawt of mi back.
Gee o'er or aahm goo'int tell mother.

Aah remember't breawn papper we used have on't bed.
Fot cover us, instead of a sheet.
It were hard fot lapse into a really deep sleep.
Cos er't rustl'in in miggle er't neet.

When it geet cowd dur'int winter.
An owd army coat was a must.
Though one thing I never werk't eawt.
Why they never cut buttons off fust.

Aah remember one story from donkeys ears sin.
When we had a posh aunty come reawnd.
So mi mam geet us gether un said lissun here.
Aah don't waant yo mek'in a seawnd.

Neaw,we had'nt bin in bed moo'er than five or ten minutes.
They had barely start'id fot eyt.
When ar Raymund poked me in't miggle er't back.
Un of course we start'id fot feight.

"Mam.... Ar Raymunds pull't th'overcoat off of the bed"
Aah sheawted deawn, with no guilt.
"It's norr an overcoat"….. mi mam whispered back.
"Whilst we've cump'ny…We caw it a quilt"

Ten minutes went by ..we were feight'in agen.
Agen aah sheawts deawn with no guilt.
"Mam…will yo come up and give him a smack.
He's just pulled the sleeve off the quilt

Th'Unsworth Dragon

In 1845 just eawtside Bury,
A likkle owd village stood.
The legend ses folk gett'n frickn'd.
Cos a dragon was maw'in abeawt in't wood.

Neaw't villagers aw geet together
Cos problum had gett'n reight dire.
So they sent off a message to London.
Fot ask for some help from this squire.

Squire Thomas Unsworth, was a local mon.
But for some reason wuz'nt abeawt.
So he travelled up north on his charger.
Wi't th'intentions of sort'in this eawt.

He were towd of this fearsome dragon.
Plagu'in aw't Th'unsworth's land.
Un be'in a recognised warrior.
Thowt he'd go up and gee um an hand.

He tackled this here dragon.
Us'in aw't tricks tharr he knew.
But at fust he could'nt mester it.
Un did'nt know worr else fot do.

Then

He gett'n a reight gradely notion.
Fot send this owd dragon to hell.
He took eawt his favorite dagger
And fitted it into his petronel.

Owd'in that gun close to his chest
Then anger'in that dragon… it's said.
Thomas shot in't throat wi that dagger.
The minnit it lifted it's yed.

Neaw with that same dagger,a table wuz carved.
Which apparantly still con be see'd.
Alung wi a few other relics
Fo't commemorate this fearless deed.

Neaw if yo gut Unsworth this village of note.
Un yo ever feel like a flaggon.
Look for the pub in the village.
The pub they named after "The Dragon "

Mi Kin

It started wi greyt grandad, Thomas.
Gradely owd fettler e wuz.
Ad'nt an hair on his yed.
Un yet ad a face full er fuzz.
He abided in Flora St, Ashton.
Born 1863
Gett'n wed to a wench cawd Eliza
Then startid their family.

Ere's greyt grandma, Eliza.
A dressmaker but it has for be said.
As a wench her neyer ad school'in.
Her at sign an X when her wed.
1883 they geet married.
Un Eliza continued fot sew.
As usual they had lots er childer
One of um, they christened him Joe.

Joe turned eawt bi mi grandfayther.
A coalminer us warked on't coal face
Loved his flat cap un his baccow.
It wuz him us wuz married to Ace
This is Esther mi grandmother,
Mi grandfayther, he cawd her "Ace"
A typical Darby un Joan they were
They even warked at same place.

1918 they geet wed.
Start'in a family proved slow.
Six childer they had, five of um dee'd
Thonely survivor was Joe.

He too turned eawt be a pitmon.
Deawn Maypow, He made a start.
Just like moo'ist miners, Joe liked a pint
Un its said he could throw a good dart

Mi dad married mi mam who wuz Ellen.
A wench us lived in't same street
Ere's a photo of Ellen
It's thonely good picture av geet.
1926 they gett'n married.
They were wed for 33 years.
Ellen turned eawt be a welder.
Un then an auxilary nurse.

Four bonney childer had Ellen and Joe
Especially chile't number three.
A nice likkle lad they cawd Jeffrey.
And Jeffrey turned eawt fot be me.
Neaw ere's me as a likkle lad.
In 1953
A lorr er waaters gone under't bridge
Since 1863.

We are going through changes

Mi Kin
Gt Grandfather (Thomas,) Gt Grandmother (Eliza,)
Grandfather (Joseph,)
Grandparents (Joseph & Esther,) Father (Joseph,)
Mother (Ellen,) & Me (Jeffrey)

Pick'in Coal

There's not much peynt in cleanin thess'ole.
Un gerr'in rid er't th'ash.
There's nowt fot mek a fire wi.
Cos mi faythers geet no cash.

Well ! corn't wi get thowd bike eawt.
Un gerr a couple er sacks.
Go on, nana, get yo clogs on.
We'll go deawn railroad tracks.

Trudgin deawn cut bank.
Bikerim in a rut.
We were both slutched up ter't th'eye baws.
We var'neer fawd in't cut.

We scrambled up ter't bankin.
Mi nana scrawped her knee.
I slorred deawn un cut mi ond.
It all'us appn't to me.

Soon wi had two sack full.
One nutty slack, un tuther wi coke.
Mi nana took it serious.
I thowt it a joke.

Her'd sling um on her showder.
Her did it on her own.
A feat, that was amazin.
Cos her weighed but seven stone.

Her'd poosh that bike awt road wom.
That too was a gradley feat.
Wi one sack slung ore't peggles.
Un tuther slung ore't seat.

It seems impossible neaw fot think.
Eaw a woman of four foot ten.
Could poosh a bike wi that much weight.
Time un time agen.

Wonc't back wom, her sowd one sack.
There allus was a buyer.
That neet wi ad some jackbit.
Un wi also ad a fire.

Faythers Day Eawt

" Eeh , owd cock, tha looks smart in yon jackit.
Them britches thi fit thi reet weel.
Just wait till tha's geet thi new cap on,
That collar, eaw does it feel ?"

Come here, al tuck thi shart lap in.
Un them draws tha's geet on , are they clen ?
Un dust know that thi flies on thi pants are undone
But tha'l at butt'n them up thi sen.

I ope tha's purr a clen vest on.
Un on thi shart tail there's nowt breawn.
Cos I don't want thi shamin mi dee'uth.
Cos remember, tha could get knocked deawn.

Neaw fass'un thi waistcoat top butt'n.
Al get thi a snotrag thats clee'un.
Un heres thi pipe un thi bacc'ow
Un theers thi specs un gowd chee'un.

They'l be waitin eawtside ert King Billy.
Hurry up Joe, tha'l at fot be doin.
If tha not theer on time, they'l go beawt thi.
So pick up thi brass un get goo'in.

Neaw when yo get Seawthpoo'ut, tak notice.
Weer charabang driver is parkin.
Un mek sure tha theer in plenty of time.
Else they'l leave thi, thal find thi sell warkin.

Neaw I know that yo'l av plenty ale.
Un last yer tha could'nt stond up.
Un tuthers thi at fotch thi wom.
On aceawnt of awt thale that thad supped.

Un when tha gets wom ,Thee be quiet.
I don't want thi mek'in a peep.
Un don't thee bi wack'nin childer.
If their wack'nt ast not gerr um sleep.

Neaw , when tha gets up in't morn mornin.
Gut lavvy afoor tha comes up.
Cos I don't want thi pee'in in't wardrobe.
Like tha's done when tha's ad too much fot sup.

So, get gone un av a good time.
I know that tha will, there's no deawt.
But mek sure owd lad, tha looks after thi sel.
Un I ope tha enjoys thi day eawt.

Photographs taken in the early 1900s in the towns of
Ashton in Makerfield and Tyldesley, both now a part
of the Borough of Wigan.

They are from a collection of family photographs and they show what life was like during the early part of the 20th century.
The street views were taken in a place locally known as "The Jig Brow" in Tyldesley.
The Jig Brow was a well known area that led down to the local colliery.
All the properties were terraced properties built by the local colliery owners.

Photographs courtesy of Barbara Unsworth

Nostalgic Memories
Translations from the Lancashire Dialect

The difference between a Lancashire Accent and the Lancashire Dialect.

Accent refers to the sounds that are present in a person's language. Therefore, if I pronounce words differently from someone, I have a different accent.
e.g. The language maybe English but spoken with a London, Yorkshire or Lancashire accent.

A dialect is a wholly different way of using the main language, not just having a different tone or accent. A dialect uses the main language, e.g. English but changes the way it puts words in order and also uses different words for things. Users of dialect would pronounce words very differently, not so much as to be another language, but enough that it would be hard for the regular language users to understand.

Lancastrians may speak with an accent but not necessarily in a dialect.

It can also be more difficult to read or understand dialect, especially by people outside of the Lancashire area.
In the Lancashire region there are many different local accents and dialects and also numerous local phrases or sayings. The poems in this particular book are written in the local

dialect that is heard around the Wigan area.

In order to allow the reader who is not from the Wigan area and who may have difficulty understanding the local dialect, I have included translations to each poem.

Please bear in mind it is not always easy to translate each word or phrase without losing the rhyme.

Jeff Unsworth

Wigan Dialect Translations.

The History of Wigan

Wigans been here a very long time.
About 2000 years or so.
The old name of Wigan was Coccium.
A name not many folk know.

The origin of Wigans a mystery.
Though we know that Romans were here.
Because when they have been digging a few holes in the road.
They have found a few things here un there
(thee,er).

The history's a bit vague around middle ages.
And the writings are not very thorough.
But we do know some time around 1246
King Henry he made it a Borough.

Now Wigan, this new Royal Borough
A proud town of houses and farms.
Reflected it's status like other big towns
And got it's own coat of arms

During the civil war the town was royalist.
Support of King Charles a matter of course.
Commander of the forces, the then Earl of Derby
Made Wigan the headquarters of the force

Now.. Parliamentry forces of Bolton.
Captured Wigan and looted through the town.
Demolishing the fortifications.
Which simply means walls were knocked down.

Cromwell himself headed troops.
In 1648.
And went into battle at Standish.
Which turned into a nasty great fight (feight).

And went into battle at Standish.
Which turned into a nasty great fight (feight).
Cromwell himself headed troops.
In 1648.

On the banks of the River Douglas.
Shed blood would leave it's stain.
It entered the local folklore.
As the Battle of Wigan Lane.

The Earl of Derby, James Stanley.
Notoriously known as Lord Strange
Was arrested and convicted of treason.
An execution was quickly arranged.

His death it occurred in Bolton
Outside of the pub Man & Scythe
There's a plaque that still marks the spot where he died.
The place where he ended his life.

Wigan also witnessed the very last act.
In the history of the Stuart cause.
When Bonny Prince Charlie after losing at Derby.
In Hallgate he stopped for a pause.

Century after century as time went on.
Wigan grew some more.
The Industrial Revolution ,
The town an open door.

Canals & Pits and factories
Springing up round here.
A town that's full of humour.
With it's famous Wigan Pier.

Many famous folk and things.
Has put Wigan on the map.
Like Orwell, Formby & Randell.
And of course the old flat cap.

Rugby League & Football
Barges filled with coal.
The Verve and Wigan Casino.
The heart of Northern Soul.

Wigan a thriving working town.
You only have to open your eyes.
A town that's known for all sorts.
Not just potato pies.

Wigan Pier

George Orwell wrote a book, you know.
The road to Wigan Pier.
He tried to tell it how it was,
how folk lived round here.

He tried to give a detailed view,
About the unemployed and poor.
He even lived amongst them all,
To help him learn some more.

He wrote about the miners.
What their work was like.
What a rotten dirty job.
Enough to make you cry. (skraahk)

Conditions not being very good,
working underground.
Hot and cramped and dusty,
With not much room for turning round.

Tunnels only three foot high,
working on their bellies. (ballys)
Picks and shovels, scraping coal,
In order to get their tallys.

They trudged home in their pit dirt,
When their shifts were done.
It was hard to tell, which was your Dad,
Black faces everyone.

Stripping off their clothes,
Getting in the tin bath.
This is when you'd see the scars,
The pit fall aftermath.

Dark black lines across their backs,
Were the coal got under the skin
The wives would scrub but never would
They be like what they'd once been.

Condemned houses, Orwell wrote.
Around the area of Scholes
Four rooms, two up two down.
Sometimes flea ridden holes

Leaking roof, walls falling down
And damp in most of the bricks
Windows wouldn't open right.
Rent six shillings, rates at three and six

Poverty was rife, Goerge Orwell wrote.
Thirty thousand claiming dole
You were glad if you even had a job.
Even digging coal

He wrote mortality was very high.
And illnesses were rife.
And generally the folk around these times
Had a really awful life.

The Story of Mab's Cross

Sir William Bradshaw of Haigh.
A knight of some renown.
Married a young girl from Blackrod and Haigh.
On the outskirts of old Wigan town.

Sir William, he had to go away.
To fight in some war.
It may have been Bannockburn.
Or it could have been further afar.

Now, it's said he was taken prisoner.
But what we don't know is, how long.
All that we know is, he never came home.
About that they can't be far wrong.

Anyway, ten years went past.
And William never came home.
And Mabel, thinking him dead.
Started seeing this other man.

Apparently, there had been a rebellion.
Against Edward the second, no doubt.
And this welshman called Osmund.
Was in his good books for helping him out.

He reakoned he'd been granted possession.
Of Haigh Hall, Well…that's what he said.
And Mabel, she had to move out.
Unless she accepted to wed.

Now… to save herself and her children.

From beggery and financial ruin.
She had to use her head and feminine wiles.
In short... just watch what she's doing.

She was forced to marry the welshman.
Lady Osmund Neville...her title.
She couldn't do anything about it
Safety of the family was vital

At the end of ten years or so.
She was giving out bread, one fine day
When one man approached,for his piece of bread
And revealed he was William of Haigh.

Now, Mabel she recognised William.
In shock, she let out a cry.
And Osmund, when he heard about it.
He grabbed her and smacked her in the eye.

Now William he bided his time.
His bite was worse than his bark.
And then he waylaid this Osmund.
And killed him outside Newton Park.

The troubles of William and Mabel.
Were not over, one has to say.
For slaying the welsh knight at Newton.
He was outlawed a year and a day.

Now, Mabel for unwitted bigamy.
Even in spite of her loss.
Had to walk barefoot from Haigh Hall to Wigan.
Each week to a place called Mab's Cross.

When his outlawry was ended.
William went back to his kin.
And when he died Mabel ordered.
A chantry building for him.

Eventually she died as well.
And in that chantry, both lay.
You can see it if you go to Wigan.
For their tombs are still there today

Mab's Cross, Wigan Lane, Wigan
The Tombs of Sir William and Lady Mabel,
Wigan Parish Church

The legend of Mab's Cross dates from 1295 when Sir William Bradshaigh married Mabel Norris de Haigh. According to the legend, William was away at war for so long, that Lady Mabel assumed him dead and married a Welsh knight, Osmond Neville.

After seven years Sir William returned, in disguise. He fought the Welsh knight at Newton Park, Newton-le-Willows and killed him there.

As penance for her unwitted bigamy, Lady Mabel walked barefoot each week from Haigh to the cross in Wigan Lane, which then became known as 'Mab's Cross'.

The stone cross probably dating from the 13th cent is located in Wigan Lane, Wigan.

The remains of the cross are a one metre square dressed gritstone block 0.57 metres (1.9 ft) high on top of a stone plinth

It was originally one of four stone crosses used as waymarkers along the medieval route from Wigan to Chorley. The cross no longer stands in its original position, having been moved across the road in 1922 as part of a road widening scheme.

The tombs of Sir William and Lady Mabel are located in Wigan Parish Church.

Hard Work

Old man, I'll have to sit down.
My legs they have nearly fell off.
My feet are both aching with running about.
And I think we have all done enough.

Whatever we do , they'll want more.
They are ruling the factory with fear.
I don't care how soon it gets to 4 o clock.
And then we can get out of here.

I've never met anyone who likes it.
And folk they keep grumbling all day.
They say that we are working our fingers to the bone.
It's not worth it for what the company pay.

But there is nothing we can do about it.
We all have to carry our load.
They have got us all over a barrel.
For no-one else pay's your road.

Posh Visitors

"We are going to have company today
Now I want you to do what your told
I don't want you messing about
But I want you be good as gold".

Aunty Winney it was that was coming
The one whose eye always flickers
Everyone thought she was posh
I reckon it's fur coat, and no knickers

Now,we hadn't much food in the pantry
So my Mam made a plate potato pie
"It'll be alright", she said, "with some carrots"
"That will be grand" answered I.

"For afters we'll have jelly and custard"
She said with her finest posh voice
"And I've made a nice singing lily
So that Winney has got a good choice".

I said, "Mam it's like having a party"
And it did look a right good pie
"Aah, well that's going to cause us a problem"
She had this sly look in her eye

"There won't be enough pie for all of us,
Cause that's all food that we've got. (gett'n)
So Jeffrey, when I ask if you want some
Say no you are not hungry, you've eaten". (ett'n)

Anyway.. the visitors sat down for their dinner.
And then the pie was brought out
I was aggravated to death
For I knew I was going to go without.

"Would you like some pie, our Jeffrey
You know it's your favorite" she said
"No Mam I'm not feeling hungry
When really, I could have eaten a flock bed

I sat there while everyone at
Thinking of nothing but the sweet
A big bowl of jelly and custard
That surely would make things alright.(awreet)

" Can I have some jelly and custard, Mam"
I asked with a glint in my eye.
"No…you can't" was the answer.
"You wouldn't eat any of the pie"

Aspirations

I'm leaving school on Friday.
I've got myself a job.
I'm starting in the smithy come Monday.
For a wage of thirty bob.

Tomorrow I'll go to the surplus store.
To get some hob nailed boots.
And then I'll want a haversack.
And one of them there boiler suits.

I didn't want to go in the factory.
And definitely not down a pit
So I've got myself an apprenticeship.
But my father, he didn't like it.

"Not as much money as they get in the factory'
you know"
And they'll take you for a fool
As soon as you have served your time.
You'll end up back in the dole queue"

"Cheap labour that's what those jobs are
I'm telling you it will come to nought (neawt).
You should have come to the Maypole pit
Where I could sort you out (eawt)"

"There's no way they will get me down the pit
Dad
I'm bound to better myself one day.
As soon as I come out of my time.
I will end up on full pay

I will have my own house one fine day.
And I'm going to have a car.
And I'll take my children for a holiday.
Somewhere further afar".

I have not had much in the way of things
And I will have to do it myself, it seems
But I've got my head screwed on correctly
And besides…I've got my dreams

Canine Wishes

The children are constantly asking for a dog you know.
Asking every day
They are plaguing me to death about it.
I shall have to give them their way.

I'm not keen on getting one myself.
You see……. I've had one before.
Chewing all the furniture.
And peeing on the floor.

It will be a novelty for a couple of weeks.
They'll be walking it about.
Then soon they'll all be sick of it.
It will be me that will have to take it out.

Dogs are not for houses…. I don't think.
Slavering all over the floor.
Dragging its backside along the rug.
And scratching on the door.

Sniffing other dogs backsides.
Then licking you on the face.
Running in when it's pouring down.
And stinking out the front place.

And then there's the cost of feeding it.
And it will have to have a ball.
I mean…them two dogs on the mantle piece
They cost nothing at all.

I will have to get Charlie Hines to dock it's tail.
Then make sure it doesn't get fits.
And then there's things like worming it.
And then all the other bits.

I will have to put my foot down.
And then that will be that.
And if they keep on crying.
I'll think about a cat.

Blast from the Past

Whilst mauling about in the yard.
Me and our kid was digging up soil with a stick.
When we found this rusty old hand grenade.
It was nestling under a brick.

"What shall we do with it"…our kid said.
We'd never seen one like it before.
We had to be quiet at this point.
For Grandad was opening the back door.

Now.. Grandad was carrying his paper.
He passed us, and gave us a smile.
We knew he was visiting the toilet.
So we knew he'd be there for a while.

We waited till he settled down.
Pushing and farting, he was.
Normally, one would keep well away.
Stinking the way that he does.

It 's a rusty old thing, this hand grenade.
As we examined this thing that we'd found.
(feawnt)
Just then our kid pulled this pin out.
Then threw it and started to count. (Ceawnt)

It rolled to the bottom of the yard.
Our kid he went white as a ghost.
It landed right near the toilet.
Where grandad was reading the post. (Local newspaper)

Our kid, he started to cry.
He'd have got the thing back if he could.
But nothing else happened for a moment.
It was then that we thought it a dud.

WHEN.....

This thing, it went off with an almighty bang.
Clouds of muck, dust and smoke….. What a state.
We both were frightened and started to run.
And then we saw grandad, hanging over the gate.

Laughing his head off, our grandad was.
And then through the laughter, he said.
" I wonder what your gran would have thought.
If I'd have let one like that go in bed".

Jeffrey's Catapult

I'm going to make a catapult this afternoon.
When I get home from school.
The elastics broken on the old one.
And I haven't much else to do.

I have seen a very good two leg.
On a tree in Leyland park.
I'm going to go down there at half past six.
As soon as it gets dark.

My dad says I've not to have one.
Because I killed a sparrow.
But he won't know that I have one.
For I'll hide it under the barrow.

I am the best shot in Higher Ince.
I can hit a can at thirty yards.
I can hit a gas lamp at fifty foot.
And the arse of the next doors cat is not so hard.

When I've got my two leg.
And two foot of square elastic.
I going to cut the tongue out of my shoe.
For this when things get drastic.

You see, I need a leather pouch.
And there's no where else to go.
So I'll have to keep hiding both my shoes.
Then my dad, he'll never know.

So now I've got the two leg.
Some elastic and the tongue out of my shoe.
Now all I need is cotton.
Any colour will do.

I will steal some out of my mothers tin.
There's no way she'll be knowing
And if she thinks theres not much left.
She will think she's used it sewing

All the ingredients now I've got
I am ready to drive folk batty
So folks watch out for Jeffrey's here.
And Jeffrey's got a catty.

Count your Blessings

It says in the Bible not to envy.
Always wanting what others have got. (geet)
To be happy with what you've been given.
And trust it will all be alright (awreet)

There is always someone worse off.
That is in a worse state than you.
We all should count our blessings.
And think, that could have been me.

There's days that we all get brassed off.
Wishing we had a bit more.
But there's plenty of folk that has nothing to eat.
And there's those who sleep on the floor.

You only have to look round about you.
It's there for everyone to see.
We all should count our blessings.
And think, that could have been me.

Whenever we feel a bit down.
Not thankful, the way that we should.
A walk round a ward down at Christies.
Would do us a right world of good.

Stop crying and think yourself lucky.
That's the right way to be.
We all should be counting our blessings
And think, that could have been me.

Cold Cure

Good heavens, I've got an headache.
I think I'm getting the flu.
I've taken a couple of Beechums.
I'm hoping that they'll do.

I tried a couple of Asprins first.
But I couldn't shake it off.
Now my nose is running.
Besides that I'm starting to cough.

All my bones are aching.
I've ulcers on my gums.
I'm going to have a whiskey.
Or else a couple of rums.

If I hadn't got false teeth.
I'd swear they all were aching.
And the wife, she has no sympathy.
She says, she cannot cope with all this noise I'm making.

She says, I should stop crying.
Which doesn't half get me riled.
She reckons, I don't know what suffering is.
Until you've had a child.

Well, I never. I've started sweating.
That rum as started to work.. I think.
So bugger all the tablets.
I'll have another drink.

Conveners Address

" Right lads, we will have a meeting"
Is usually the shout.
"We have got a bit of business.
We have to get sorted out"

All the lads they start to gather.
The meetings on the go.
Then you hear those famous words.
"Right lads…As you know"

The meetings called to order.
And soon gets under way.
And then the convener tells us.
We are on about our pay.

" How much are they offering"
One mans heard to shout.
" Is it what we asked for.
Or are we coming out"

"Now, calm down chaps.
There's no talk of us striking.
Lets consider what they've offered.
Before we all start skraak'in. (crying)

I'll read just what they've offered.
But I want you to keep your cool.
And if you don't like what you hear.
We can always's work to rule"

Little Jim

Good heavens.. it looks a sight (seet)
Down that Shuttle street.
Chances of getting it clean is rather slim.
With only one sweeper … little Jim.

It's funny it's not made him bitter.
How folk keep throwing down their litter.
But he keeps going from year to year.
Mind you .. that's what they pay him for.

Walking down in the morning,
After Sunday night.
You want to see all the paper.
Doesn't half look a sight.

Especially if it's windy,
Making it look worse.
But Jimmy never bothers.
You never hear him curse.

He carries on from day to day.
With his spade and little brush.
Going along at an even pace.
And never in a rush.

It's morning Mary..
How you doing Bob.
And then he gets his head down.
And carries on with the job..

Missing the Old Cock

"Whats up with you mother.
Has something got you down.
You look like you've found a threepenny bit
And lost a half a crown".

"I'm just sat here on my own
Thinking about the old lad.
I wish the old cock was here now.
Then things wouldn't seem so bad.

I used to get on at him, you know.
For breaking wind and stinking.
I would give anything now, to hear him fart.
And I wouldn't mind him drinking.

I'd love to be tucking his shirt lap in his drawers.
And making sure his fly was done up.
And taking him to bed when he got home at night.
All them times he'd had too much to sup.

I wouldn't complain about muck on his lap
Or the snot that was all down his sleeve.
Or in the latter days when he pee'd down his leg.
I just wish he didn't have to leave.

I wish he was here with us now.
And then I could kiss his bald head.
All the things I wish I'd have told him.
But now it's too late to be said.

It doesn't seem two minutes since he popped his clogs
Like Darby and Joan we used to be.
And now…when I think about the old lad.
I wish the Lord would take me.

Now, come on mother, buck yourself up.
Dwelling on it is bound to be upsetting
And you know just what my father would say.
Now, Esther, you stop your fretting.

He wouldn't want you sat here moping.
You know just what he'd say.
Come on our Ace. Get off your arse.
And make us a nice cup of tea (tay).

Washing My Hair

I think I'll wash my hair tonight.
It's getting full of dirt.
It's full of muck and dandruff.
It's falling on my shirt.

I don't like looking scruffy.
So while I've got the time.
I'll give my hair a right good scrub.
And hang it on the line.

Nip in the Air

"Good morning lad's, it's not so warm".
Is usually the greeting.
When the workers enter Golstones.
And the place it still wants heating.

"Better to leave your coat on.
Until you've had a drink.
And then we'll see the shop steward.
And he can cause a stink.

Our lads won't work in this cold".
Will be the plea from him.
When really it's not that bad.
Well .. not for working in.

Within an hour it soon gets warm.
And so you see , it shows.
A little bit of awkwardness.
Will keep them on their toes.

Visiting My Gran

I always visited on a Saturday.
To do the shopping for my gran.
Platt Bridge was a long way for children.
On the trollybus from the bird ith hand.

It seemed a long way in those days.
When you are nine or ten.
But two and sixpence was too much to miss.
You could buy allsorts for threepence back then.

Now .. I couldn't abide peeling potatoes.
As a child it did get me down.
But my father he said I must do it.
If I wanted to get half a crown.

Sometimes I'd stay overnight.
It was great when it came time for bed.
We'd climb up the stairs with a candle.
Which flickered on fathers bald head.

We'd all have a pee in the jerry.
Which was quickly shoved under the bed.
You could smell it in the night if you woke.
But nothing about it was said.

We'd lie there with the candle flickering.
Making shadows and shapes on the wall. (war)
And we'd play at trying to find faces.
On the damp patches that we all saw.

When the time came for me to be going.
My gran said…. Joe treat that lad.
But my father he always plagued me.
Which used get my grandmother mad.

He'd sit on a chair with his back to the fire
His braces were dangling on the floor
He'd say… Jeffries come pull my finger
Then fart, and I'd run through the door.

He'd give me the money , I'd kiss him on his head
My grandmother saw me to the door
I'd kiss her on the cheek ,she gave me a hug.
I'd say.. " thanks , and I'll see you some more".

Hell To Pay (Toupee)

It started with a bald spot.
About as big as half a crown.
Then it got much bigger.
And worked it's way around.

Everytime I had a bath.
Or washed my hair at night (neet)
I 'd look down onto the floor
There would be hair all round my feet.

Falling out in chunks it was.
Bald as a coot on top.
And then I tried a toupee.
It looked just like a mop.

I said I wouldn't wear it.
The wife said it looked all right
I said that folk would laugh at me
Because it looked a sight.

She got her way, I wore it.
It was stuck on with tape and pinned.
But everybody laughed at me.
It blew off in the flipp'in wind.

*This Poem was the winning poem in the
Leigh Festival of Arts Dialect Poetry
Competition 1996
(Humorous Section)*

Scissors, Combs and Pencils

I can't find those scissors.
I've been looking for an hour. (har)
Has any of you lot seen them.
They can't have gone so far.

There once were thirteen pair in this house.
Kept in that sideboard.
Just wait until I find them .
I'll hide them out of the road.

It is same with combs and pencils.
There's always falling out.
For when you come to want one.
There's never none about.

Someone will suffer one day.
You'll hear them shout out … ouch.
Then you'll know the've found them.
They'll be right down the back of the couch.

Very Good Food

It's hard to understand dialect.
It will surprise me if you can.
For there's certain things that's said round here.
You can't make head or tail on.

How can you expect a southerner.
That is in a queue with us.
Understand when someone asks.
For two and a half pound of potatoes.

Now folk up north are good folk.
And by God they know how to eat.
For the old ones teach all the young ones.
How to cook a piece of meat.

There's tripe and brawn and wesson.
Lambs fry and savoury duck.
There's cow heel and sometimes a nice sheeps head.
With the legs with any luck.

There's elder, pigs cheek and trotters.
Oxtail and a nice bit of tongue.
But it's mostly the old ones that eat it.
They won't touch it when they're young.

Today they know nothing about cooking.
They get it all out of a can.
Or else they're defrosting a packet.
The old way's of cooking are gone.

In the old days, nothing got wasted.
Ballyhand day was the middle of the week.
All the leftovers were thrown into a large frying pan.
And came out as bubble and squeak.

Toad in the hole,lobbies and broth.
Or baking all through the night. (neet)
Food that went a long way.
Was the answer to making ends meet

You couldn't blame them really
It was hard to make the ends meet
They did their best with what they could get.
And most were run off they're feet.

I look back now to those days.
And although there wasn't always meat.
I remember there was always food.
We always had something to eat.

Going to the Baths

It was good going to the baths on a Saturday
Three or four of us waiting for the bus.
As soon as it came, we'd all fight get on.
Because all of us wanted to be first.

Now someone always forgot something.
A towel, there'd be a fair chance.
But we never forgotten our swimtrunks.
For we had them on under our pants.

Before the bus stopped, top of King Street.
We'd jump off for we couldn't wait.
We'd run through grimses arcade.
Cross Library Street, into Millgate.

Now... by this time we'd all be excited.
Racing to the bottom of the slope.
Then rush through the door, we'd all get that
whiff
Of chlorine and carbolic soap.

Three of us squashed in one cabin.
Getting undressed stood on the seat.
Then rushing down the steps, into the showers.
Lathering our trunks and scrubbing our feet.

I got threw out once for pee'ing in the pool.
The attendant he pushed me into the road.
I said.. it wasn't right that most people pee.
He said... not off the top diving board.

Now… they would make us leave about four.
We would wonder where the time, it had gone.
We would call at a shop for an hovis brown loaf.
Eat the middle out , as we walked home.

The Holidays

I'm glad it's got to the holidays.
I'm just about getting sick.
I can't say it's the rest I'm needing.
But a break for a couple of week.

I shall be rushing off to blackpool.
In to a nice hotel as a guest.
But I guess when the fortnights over.
I'll be glad to get back to work for the rest.

I hope we get good weather.
But it'll probably rain all week. (wik)
Then the kid's will all be crying.
We'll all be getting sick.

Then the wife will pull a face.
And wish we hadn't come.
And then I'll probably lose my cool.
And take them all back home.

Shilling for Cleaning

Right… We are going to clean through the house today.
I want the whole place clean.
Your not going playing till it's been done.
So I hope you all know what I mean.
Now Raymond, you do the toilet
Get the Lanry from under the sink.
And make sure you scrub under the rim.
It's that what's been causing that stink.

Terence, you do the grate.
Give it a right good black leading.
And make sure you clean inside the oven.
Even if you have to get your head in.
Scrape all those ashes from under the grate.
Then open that new bundle of sticks.
Screw up some paper to make a good fire.
For your dad will be home about six.

Jeffrey.. you can do the kitchen.
And don't forget to stone that step.
There's a new donkey brand under the slop stone.
And you know were the mop rags are kept.
I shall be filling the dollytub.
There's a great pile of washing needs doing.
So while I'm in the wash house, no falling out.
Now pick up your things and get going.

The Only Solution

Nineteen years old and sat in the house.
It's not her fault she can't get a job.
The situation is she's willing to take anything.
Just to earn a few bob.

It can't do much good for kids of her age.
Sitting for hours, writing page after page.
Applying for this and applying for that.
Then hearing she's been turned down flat.

It makes you wonder what's going on.
And what theyr'e going to do.
They keep on saying educate.
They have to stay on at school.

The way that I understand it.
There's only one thing to do.
That's lowering the retirement age.
Down to twenty two.

Hometime at Golstones

Get out of the way , theyre coming.
At half past three they shout.
It's murder if your caught in the rush.
When the women's coming out.

All that bumping weight .
Fighting to get to the front.
There's one there, must be twenty stone.
Looks like an elephant.

If you get in the way of that girl.
Underneath those legs.
You'll end up in Leigh infirmary.
As sure as eggs are eggs.

So take a tip from one that knows.
And listen to this line.
Try to get out before them.
Or work some overtime.

What a Palava

What a palava at bedtime.
Three grown up folk and four children.
Two double beds and one single
No wonder my mam was bewildered.

Now my Nana she had the little bed.
And my Mam and my Dad had a double.
That left only one more for the children.
And that's why we had all this trouble.

We tried all roads to sleep with some comfort.
Length ways and cross ways we'd lie.
There were elbows and legs all over the show
It were easy to get poked in your eye.

"Stop turning over" one would shout out.
"Give me some blanket" cried another.
Get your elbow out of my back.
Give over or I'm going to tell mother.

I remember brown paper we used have on the bed.
To cover us, instead of a sheet.
It were hard to lapse into a really deep sleep.
Because of the rustling in the middle of the night
(neet.)

When it got cold in the winter.
An old army coat was a must.
Though one thing I never worked out.
Why they never cut the buttons off first.(fust)

Now we hadn't been in bed more than five or ten minutes.
They had barely started to eat
Then our Raymond poked me in the middle of my back
And of course we started to fight. (feight)

"Mam…. Our Raymond has pulled the overcoat off of the bed
I shouted down, with no guilt
"It's not an overcoat"….. my Mam whispered back.
"Whilst we've company…We call it a quilt"

Ten minutes went by ..we were fighting again.
Again I shout down with no guilt.
"Mam…will you come up and give him a smack.
He's just pulled the sleeve off the quilt"

The Unsworth Dragon

In 1845 just outside Bury
A little old village stood.
The legend says folk got quite frightened.
For a dragon was lurking about in the wood.

Now, the villagers they all got together
For the problem had become dire.
So they sent off a message to London.
To ask for some help from this squire.

Squire Thomas Unsworth, was a local.
But for some reason he wasn't about.
So he travelled up north on his charger.
With the intentions of sorting this out.

He was told of this fearsome dragon.
Plaguing the Unsworth's land.
And being a recognized warrior.
Thought he'd go up and give them a hand.

He tackled this here dragon.
Using all of the tricks that he knew.
But at first he couldn't master it.
And didn't know what else to do.

Then

He got a right excellent idea.
That would send this old dragon to hell.
He took out his favorite dagger
And fitted it into his petronel.

Holding that gun close to his chest
Then angering that dragon… it's said.
Thomas shot in the throat with that dagger.
The moment it lifted it's head.

Now… with that same dagger a table was carved
Which apparently still can be seen. (seed)
Along with a few other relic
To commemorate this fearless deed

Now if you go to Unsworth…. this village of note
And you ever feel like a flaggon
Look for the pub in the village.
The pub they named after "The Dragon "

My Kin

It started with my great grandad, Thomas.
Nice old man, he was
Hadn't an hair on his head.
And yet had a face full of fuzz.

He abided in Flora St, Ashton.
Born 1863
Got wed to a girl called Eliza
Then started their family.

Here's great grandma, Eliza.
A dressmaker but it has to be said.
As a girl she never had schooling.
She had to sign an X when she wed.

1883 they got married.
And Eliza continued to sew.
As usual they had lots of children.
One of them, they christened him Joe.

Joe turned out be my grandfather.
A coalminer that worked the coal face
Loved his flat cap and tobacco.
It was him that was married to Ace

This is Esther my grandmother,
My grandfather, he called her "Ace"
A typical Darby and Joan they were
They even worked at same place

1918 they got married.
Starting a family proved slow.
Six children they had, five of them died.
The only survivor was Joe.

My dad married my mam who was Ellen.
A girl that lived in the same street
Here's a photo of Ellen
It's the only good picture I've got. (geet)

1926 they got married.
They were married for 33 years.
Ellen turned out to be a welder.
And then an auxiliary nurse.

Four lovely children had Ellen and Joe.
Especially the child, number three.
A nice little boy they called Jeffrey.
And Jeffrey turned out to be me.

Now here's me as a little boy.
In 1953.
A lot of waters gone under the bridge
Since 1863

Picking Coal

There's not much point in cleaning the ashes.
And getting rid of the trash.
There is nothing to make a fire with.
For my dad has got no cash.

Well, can't we get the bike out.
And get a couple of sacks.
Go on Nana, get your clogs on.
We'll go down to the railway tracks.

Walking down the canal bank.
The bike rim in a rut.
We were both muddied up to the eyeballs.
We nearly fell in the cut. (canal)

We scrambled up the banking.
My Nana scraped her knee.
I slipped down and cut my hand.
It always happened to me.

Soon we had two sacks full.
One nutty slack and one with coke.
My Nana took it serious.
I thought it a joke.

She would sling them on her shoulder.
She did it on her own.
A feat that was amazing.
She weighed but seven stone.

She pushed the bike all the way home.
That too, a very good feat.
With one sack over the peddles.
And the other over the seat.

It seems impossible now to think.
How a woman of four foot ten.
Could push a bike with all that weight
Time and time again

Once back home, she sold one sack
There always was a buyer
That night we had some food.
We also had a fire.

Fathers Day Out

Old man, you look smart in that jacket.
Those trousers, they fit you very well (weel)
Just wait till you've got your new hat on.
That new collar, how does it feel.
Come here , I'll tuck your shirt tail in.
Those underpants you've got on, are they clean.
(clen)
And do you know that the flies on your pants are undone.
But you'll have to button those up your self. (sen)

I hope that youve put a clean vest on.
And on your shirt tail there's nothing brown.
For I don't want you shaming me to death.
For remember you could get knocked down.
Now fasten your waistcoat top button.
I'll get you a hankie thats clean.
And here's your pipe and your tobacco.
And there is your specs and gold chain.

They'll be waiting outside the King Billy.
Hurry up Joe you'll have to be doing.
If your not there on time, they'll go without you.
So pick up your money and get going.
Now when you get to Southport, take notice.
Where the coach driver is parking.
And make sure that your there in plenty of time.
Or they'll leave you, you'll find yourself walking

Now I know that you'll have plenty ale.
And last year you couldn't stand up.
The others they had to bring you home.
On account of the ale that you'd supped.
Now when you get home, you be quiet.
I don't want you making a peep
And don't you be wakening the children
If they're awakened I won't get them to sleep.

And when you get back in the morning
Go to the toilet before you come up
And I don't want you peeing in the wardrobe.
Like you've done when you've had to much to sup.
So get gone and have a good time.
I know that you will, there's no doubt.
But make sure old lad you look after yourself.
And I hope you enjoy the day out.

.

*The winning poem in the
Leigh Festival of Arts Dialect Poetry Competition 1996
(Humorous Section)*

"El Toopay"

Phrases & Sayings

Eaw fot speyk reet
There are many expressions in the Lancashire Dialect
that end with the word "tuh".
.ie - Ar'tuh …" Tha not goo'in Ar'tuh.".."
You're not going . Are you ?"

Wuz'tuh …" Tha wer'nt wi um, Wuz'tuh."..
" You was'nt with them, Was you ?"

Con'tuh … " Tha con do it, Con'tuh."..
" You can do it ,Can't you ?"

Wil'tuh … " Cotch owd er that, Wil'tuh."..
" Catch hold of that,Will you ?"

Duz'tuh… " Tha does'nt like it, Duz'tuh…
" You don't like it, Do you?"

As'tuh... " Tha's not done it agen...As'tuh?"
" You hav'nt done it again... Have you?"

Other words

Cor'nt….. Cannot.
Wain't….. Will not.
Maun't…. Must not.
Darn't….. Dare not.
Art'nt….. Are you not.
Will't….. Will you.

In the Lancashire dialect somehow "dd" becomes "gg"
Eg… He's ett'n miggle eawt un left or't theawtsides.
He has eaten the middle out and left all the outsides.

Mi yeds aw muggl't up.
My head is in a muddle.

Am beawn't bey a new moggle.
I am going to buy a new model.

Hers figglin't books.
She is fiddling the books.

Eaw't diggl'in.
How are you diddling (how are you doing)

Tha't puggl't thee.
Your puddled you. (your not so bright)

Stop thi meggl'in.
Stop your meddling. (Don't play around with that)

Somehow double "TT" becomes "ck"

EG.. As't feckl't it.

Have you fettled it. (Have you mended it)
Neaw seckle deawn.
Now settle down.

There are also numerous expressions that don't make sense .

.ie..Mothers expressions to children, that made a child wonder
if their mother had lost the plot.

" Does thaa know who tha talkin to?"
"Do you know who you are talking to"?

" Who dust think tha are?"
"Who do you think you are"?

" Who dust think I am ?"
"Who do you think I am"?

" As't seen er't back of thi ears?"
"Have you seen at the back of your ears"?

" Just tak a scen ert back of thi neck."
"Just look at the back of your neck"?

" Neaw ! Come on, Gerr off."

"Now, come on, get off"

" Does tha know who I am."

" If tha faw's off yon war un breyks thi legs, don't come runnin to me."

"If you fall off that wall and break your legs, don't come running to me"

Local Sayings

Local seyins.

" as't knock that smile on ter't tuther side er thi face"
I will knock that smile to the other side of your face.

" Don't thee threeup me eawt"…..
Don't you keep answering back

" Who's let polly eawt er prison"…. ?
Which one of you has broke wind?

Her's as feaw as a clog back.
Her'd frick'n a police horse
Her fa'yers a bulldog chewin a wa'sp.
She's not very good looking.

Am powfagged un jigger't
I'm extremely exhausted .

Am clem't dee'uth
Mi bally thinks mi throats cut.
Aah could e'yt a scabby pigAah could e'yt a flock bed
I'm very hungry

Her's norr as far through as a kipper.
There's moo'er meyt on a butchers brat
She's rather thin.

Her's not maw'in beawt
She's got quite large ones.

Her con fradge till ceaws come wom
She can talk till the cows come home.

Yon mons as bent as an arubs dagger
That man is not very honest.

Her skens like a basket er whelks…
That ladies eyes meet in the middle.

Bat thisell abeawt a bit
Could you make yourself useful.

Tha't backerts thee
Your not very bright.

Tha't not backerts at com'in forr'erts
Your quite forward.

Tharr ars'in abeawt like a mon beawt legs
Your taking too much time.

Yon babbies skraakin it's yed off
The baby is crying.

Wot yelpin at
Why are you crying.

I corn't keep mi een opp'n
I can't stay awake.

Win fawd eawt
We are not speaking.

As't mollycrush thi
I will give you a beating.

There's nowt spaa,lin….. (It can wait.)
Tha's sheeded it.
Tha's keck't it o'er
You have spilled it.

" Who are thy thee'in thee…
Si thee , Don't thee thee me thee.

" Tha's gett'n a face like a smacked arse"
"You are looking quite down in the dumps".

" Geritt ett'n"
Would you eat it please.

" Her fotch't it aw back"
I'm afraid she's been sick.

Win bowt a six leet ark'nin device…..
We have got a wireless

Greetings

Eawt goo'in on serry
How are you going on.

Am fain sithee
I'm glad to see you.

Ar'tor' reet
Are you well.

Neaw owd cock'er.. sit thi deawn
now old man.. sit yourself down.

Swant a brew
Would you care for a cup of tea.

Words

Dialect Words

AGATE :- Her's gerr'in agate er mi (She is getting on at me)

AGATE :- He's gett'n agate caw'in for mi. (He has got in the habit of calling for me)

Origin:- Old Norse word Gata

....

ACS :- "Acs him worr he waants" " ask him what he wants"

Old English ACSIAN to ask
or enquire

....

AWOVARUCK "Ther front room looked weel, it was awovaruck"" Their front room looked well, it was very untidy"

They wer feight'in aw of a ruck.

....

BLETHERYED :- He's a reight Bletheryed (A person who is not very bright)

Old Norse BLATHRA

....

BANT :-"Mi jackets bin'ter't cleaners un thiv tack'n awt bant eawt of it"

"My jacket has been to the cleaners and it does'nt have the same quality as before"

....

BRAT :-"Thall need't wear a brat " (an apron)

PINNY :- also an apron

....

CACK :- "Mam, aahm goo'in forr a cack" (Mother I am going to the toilet)

Also CACK handed (Left handed person)

....

CALE :- Keep thi cale in't queue. (Keep your turn in the queue)

Don't lerr um cale thi. (don't let them push in front of you)

CLEMT or CLEMMED :- Aahm clemt dee'uth (I am very hungry)

CRACK ON :- Her knew summut burr her neyer cracked on. (She knew something but she never said a word)

DEG :- Aah mon deg mi plants or thill dee. (I must water my plants or they will die)

Norwegian :- Deggja

EEN :- Aah mon get mi een tested (I must get my eyes tested)

ESSHOLE :- Aah'l at clen th'esshole eawt. (I will have to clean under the fire grate)

Probably stems from ASHOLE

THREEUP :- To try to get one better than someone.
(Stop three'upping)

FRADG'IN :- Gossiping.
(Watt'ch them theer wimm'in fradg'in) (Watch those women gossiping)

....

WENCH'IN :- Going after the girls.
....

BALLYWARCH :- Belly ache.
YEDWARCH :- Headache
TH'EARWARCH :- Earache.

....
PETTY :- Outside Lavatory.

....

THRUTCH'IN :- Struggling to pass a motion on the toilet.

....

MEEMAW'IN :- Try to get someone to understand what you are saying by the use of facial expressions and hand language.

....

Old Potographs

Down the Jig. Tyldesley

The Jig or Jig brow was a collection of terraced rows in the town of Tyldesley nicknamed (Bongs) near Manchester.They ran along Manchester road, down to the railway line on the border of Astley. Only a few of these houses still stand today.

One of these terraced rows was called Greenbank St. This is where these street scenes were taken.The railway line ran from the direction of Leigh, through Tyldesley and then on to Manchester.

The land rises up from Astley to the railway banks.The banks then became known as Bongs.In this picture of one of the numerous local football teams, you can see the railway sidings.

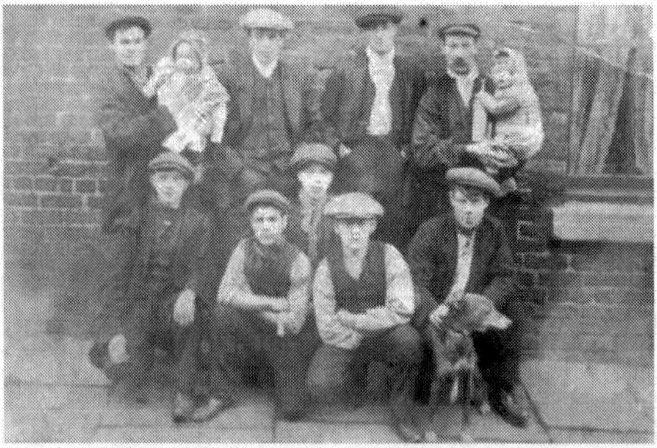

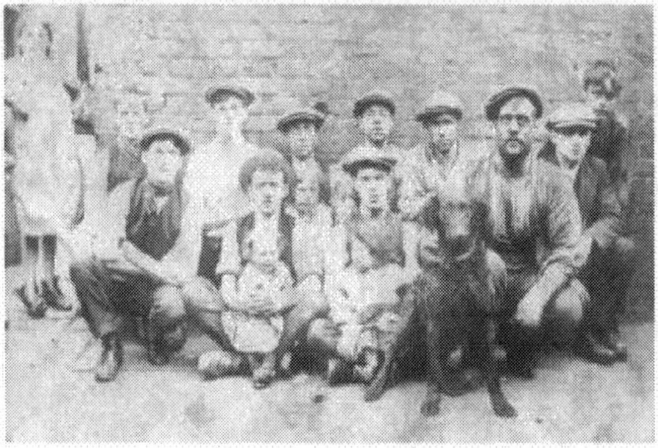

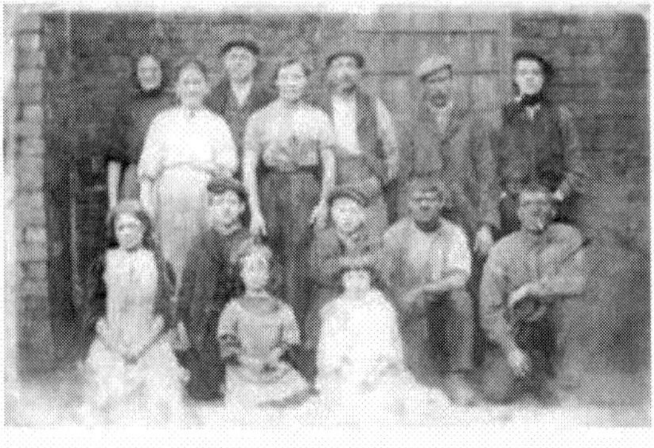

Street scenes
Greenbank Street, Tyldesley.
An area called "Jig Brow"

Photos of Local People & Styles of Dress

133

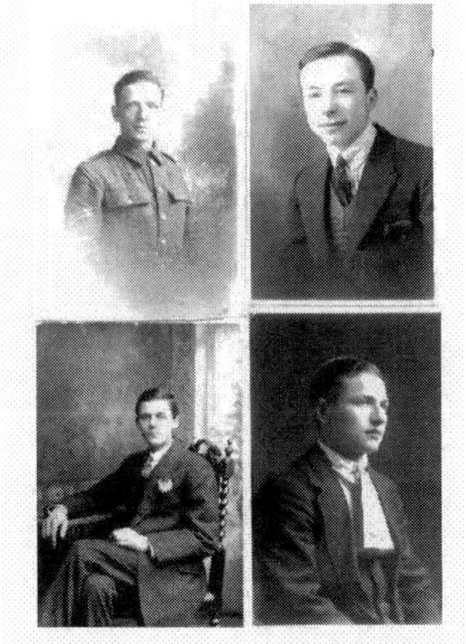

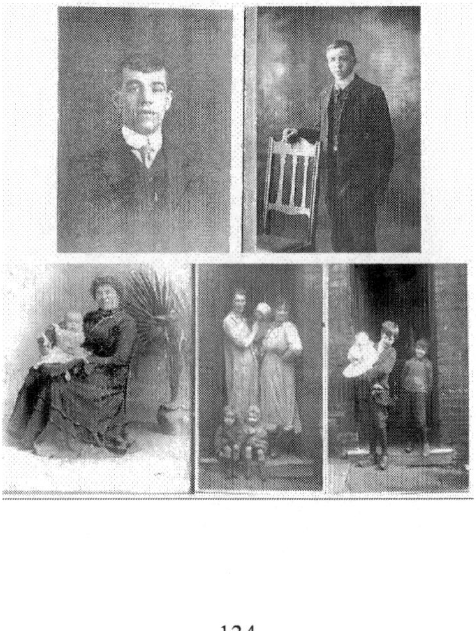

Items of Interests
Wiggin,Leyth,Bent & Bongs.
Wigan,Leigh,Atherton & Tyldesley.

The Tyldesley Ox Roasting

Once a year in Tyldesley an Ox roasting was held.
This event was held on Shackerly Common.
Here is an old photograph. Date unknown

Here are two more Photo's of The Ox Roasting
dated 1955
Photograph's courtesy of John Edwards
The Butchers were D J Edwards & Billy Wrend

Here is one of the greaseproof bags that was used to serve pieces of the roasted ox.

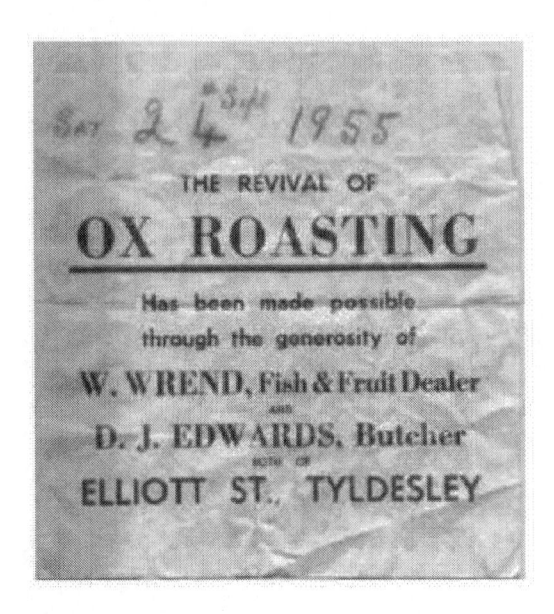

> Sat 24th 1955
> THE REVIVAL OF
> **OX ROASTING**
> Has been made possible through the generosity of
> **W. WREND, Fish & Fruit Dealer**
> and
> **D. J. EDWARDS, Butcher**
> both of
> **ELLIOTT ST., TYLDESLEY**

The Great Vicar of Tyldesley
The Reverend John Lund, MA.

St Georges, Tyldesley Parish Church
Here is a photograph of the memorial plaque that is situated in the St Georges Church in Tyldesley.

John Lund was the vicar in Tyldesley from 1884-1924
I found this photograph in a house in Shuttle St, Tyldesley.
I purchased the property in 1972.
The house was built by Caleb Wright the mill owner in 1825 for a man named William Ramsden who owned the Nelson Colliery in Tyldesley.
Both Caleb Wright and William Ramsden were very prominent in the local town hall.
From one of the front windows, William Ramsden could see the windings of the colliery.
The Reverend John Lund married William Ramsdens daughter Susan and lived in the house for a time.
The house was built in the georgian style and had six bedrooms, it had four rooms in a cellar it also had a detached stable.
In the cellars, instead of using the usual wooden joists, railway lines from the Nelson colliery over on Shackerley Common were used. All the outer walls were solid four brick thick walls. All the windows were panelled in rosewood and it had a lovely rosewood winding staircase.
In 1889 the detached property was divided into two separate houses and a further two houses added, making a terraced row.

You can see the original house (the two houses on the right) in this photograph,

The house had iron railings originally (obviously taken for use in the war effort)

The house also had 3 rooms in the cellars, 2 had fire places.
It also had gardens to the rear of the property.
There was a natural spring in the gardens and it is said that the locals used to bring horses to drink from it.
When the other houses were built round about the property, the spring was blocked up and eventually found a new route. The water came up into the cellar of the house.
I eventually had the water tested and it was found pure, I proceeded to make lots of fruit wines using this water.

<<<<<<<<<<<[>>>>>>>>>>

Printed in Great Britain
by Amazon